CW01651851

FlashRevise Pocketbook

AS/A-Level Physical Education

Skills Acquisition
& Sports Psychology

Philip Allan Updates, an imprint of Hodder Education, an Hachette UK company, Market Place, Deddington, Oxfordshire OX15 0SE

Orders

Bookpoint Ltd, 130 Milton Park, Abingdon, Oxfordshire OX14 4SB
tel: 01235 827720 fax: 01235 400454 e-mail: uk.orders@bookpoint.co.uk

Lines are open 9.00 a.m.–5.00 p.m., Monday to Saturday, with a 24-hour message answering service. You can also order through our website: www.philipallan.co.uk

ISBN 978-1-4441-1545-1

First printed 2010

Impression number 5 4 3 2 1
Year 2014 2013 2012 2011 2010

Printed in Spain

P01744

Skills Acquisition

Sports Psychology

Skill I

Q1 State three characteristics of a skilled movement.

Q2 At what stage of learning is a highly skilled performer?

Q3 What do cognitive skills involve?

Q4 Why are perceptual skills important when taking part in a sporting activity?

ANSWERS

the learned ability to bring about predetermined results with maximum certainty

A1 Choose from: consistent; efficient; coordinated; fluent; goal-orientated; recognisable

A2 Autonomous stage/phase

A3 Mental processes, such as problem solving and devising tactics and strategies to overcome an opponent

A4 They allow us to interpret the information entering our bodies, which affects our decisions on how to deal with the situation

***examiner's* note** When asked for an example to illustrate your answer, be specific. Don't just name a sport; give a definite skill or situation. For example, if asked to name a situation where a perceptual skill may be used, rather than state 'hockey' as your response, write 'dribbling with the ball'.

Skill II

Q1 What is a motor skill?

Q2 Name the type of skill that involves no interference from the local environment.

Q3 Name the type of skill that has a clear beginning and end.

Q4 What is a self-paced skill?

ANSWERS

the learned ability to bring about predetermined results with maximum certainty

A1 A skill that involves movement, e.g. a smash in badminton

A2 Closed skill; the action remains the same each time it is performed, in a stable, unchanging environment, e.g. a gymnastic vault, a javelin throw or a swimming racing dive

A3 Discrete skill, e.g. a tennis serve, a basketball free-throw or a place-kick in rugby

A4 A skill that involves the performer having control over the movement in terms of its speed and timing of execution, e.g. athletics throwing events, the service in a racket sport or diving off a springboard

***examiner's* note** When asked to place a skill on a continuum, make sure you give a reason to justify your answer.

Skill III

Q1 Name the type of skill that has several discrete elements or subroutines linked together to form an integrated sequence.

Q2 What is an open skill?

Q3 Name the type of skill that involves large muscle movement during its execution.

Q4 Outline the characteristics of a complex skill.

ANSWERS

A1 Serial skill, e.g. a gymnastics routine, a triple jump or a basketball lay-up shot

A2 A skill directly influenced by the local environment, which is unstable, changing and unpredictable; the performer must be aware of positions and options, constantly determining and altering the rate and timing of execution of the skill

A3 Gross skill

A4 It requires conscious thought during its execution in order to control and make adjustments as necessary

***examiner's* note** Make sure you can explain clearly the key characteristics of each continuum.

Skill IV

Q1 Name the type of skill that has no definite beginning or end.

Q2 What is a fine skill?

Q3 Outline the characteristics of a simple skill.

Q4 What is an externally paced skill?

ANSWERS

the learned ability to bring about predetermined results with maximum certainty

A1 Continuous skill, e.g. running, cycling and swimming

A2 A skill that involves the performer completing accurate, precise movements using small muscle groups

A3 Basic movement patterns; little decision making; completed with minimum conscious control

A4 A skill that involves the performer reacting to changing environmental conditions, with little control over the rate and timing of the movement, e.g. receiving a tennis serve, catching a pass or white-water rafting

***examiner's* note** It is unlikely that you will be required to provide a specific definition of skill, but you must be able to give a full description, and outline characteristics of, a skilled movement.

Ability I

Q1 What is the difference between skill and ability?

Q2 What is psychomotor/perceptual motor ability?

Q3 What is gross motor ability?

Q4 Why are abilities task-specific?

ANSWERS

an inherited, innate trait that allows an individual to complete various tasks

A1 Skill is learnt; ability is innate

A2 Ability that involves the processing of information and the initiation of movement, e.g. coordination and reaction time

A3 Ability that involves actual movement, e.g. flexibility, strength, stamina and speed

A4 In order to achieve success, each skill requires different types of ability or may require similar abilities, but to differing degrees of importance

***examiner's* note** Make sure you can explain the difference between skill and ability, as well as the relationship between them.

Ability II

Q1 State three gross motor abilities required to excel in the sport of high jumping.

Q2 State three psychomotor abilities required to play netball.

Q3 Explain why the concept of 'natural athletic ability' is largely a myth.

Q4 Name a common test used to measure agility.

ANSWERS

an inherited, innate trait that allows an individual to complete various tasks

A1 Choose from: explosive strength; speed; flexibility; dynamic balance

A2 Choose from: reaction time; coordination; manual dexterity; aiming; response orientation

A3 Abilities have to be developed and refined in order to execute skills; performers only appear to have natural athletic ability when their ability has been developed sufficiently to make the skill look effortless and natural

A4 Illinois agility run

***examiner's* note** When asked to 'list' or 'state' a specific number of abilities, don't just write a long list and hope for the best. The examiner may only take those at the beginning of your list.

Learning I

Q1 What is the difference between learning and performance?

Q2 What is the S–R bond?

Q3 'Insight' or 'gestalt' theories are .... theories of learning.

Q4 Operant conditioning can also be referred to as .... and .... learning.

ANSWERS

the relatively permanent change in behaviour that occurs as a direct result of experience

A1 Learning is permanent; performance is a temporary occurrence

A2 The stimulus–response bond; the relationship between a stimulus and the specific action that it initiates

A3 Cognitive

A4 Trial and error

***examiner's* note** You should be able to relate the theories of learning to practical examples.

Learning II

Q1 What is associationist learning theory?

Q2 When discussing learning, what is a performer's drive?

Q3 What is operant conditioning?

Q4 .... reinforcement increases the likelihood of an action being repeated.

ANSWERS

the relatively permanent change in behaviour that occurs as a direct result of experience

A1 A theory based on the performer developing a relationship between a stimulus and a response

A2 The performer's level of motivation to achieve a specific goal

A3 The coach manipulates the environment to shape the actions of the performer and uses reinforcement either to strengthen or to weaken the S–R bond, depending on the outcome

A4 Positive

***examiner's* note** You should be able to explain the advantages and disadvantages of each theory of learning in terms of developing performance.

Learning III

Q1 What is the drive reduction theory?

Q2 What term refers to the withdrawal of an adverse stimulus that strengthens the S–R bond?

Q3 Suggest two ways a teacher/coach may manipulate the environment to develop a specific action or behaviour pattern.

Q4 What is the major difference between cognitive and operant-conditioning theories of learning?

ANSWERS

the relatively permanent change in behaviour that occurs as a direct result of experience

A1 Learning takes place if performers are motivated to complete the task and reduce their drive; following success, a new challenge has to be set

A2 Negative reinforcement

A3 Choose from: restrict working areas; break down skills into subroutines for practice; give verbal cues; devise specific practice to restrict options available; trial-and-error practice

A4 Cognitive theory involves the performer understanding the relationship between the stimulus and the response and making appropriate adjustments; operant conditioning only requires the performer to complete a specific sequence

***examiner's* note** You need to understand the link between motivation and learning.

Learning IV

Q1 What is the purpose of punishment when referring to operant conditioning?

Q2 .... theory suggests people learn by observing others and then copying their actions.

Q3 What is a significant other? Give two examples.

Q4 Models are often used to aid learning. Give three factors that may enhance their effectiveness.

ANSWERS

the relatively permanent change in behaviour that occurs as a direct result of experience

A1 To weaken the S–R bond/behaviour and reduce the likelihood of a reoccurrence

A2 Social learning

A3 A person of high status in the opinion of the performer; examples include role models, teachers, coaches, parents and peer-group and family members

A4 Choose from: similar in ability to improve confidence; high status; appropriate behaviour links to expected norms; consistency of behaviour; relevant actions; reinforcement of behaviour; highly skilled and successful; friendly

***examiner's* note** Make sure you understand the difference between reinforcement and punishment.

Learning V

Q1 What is vicarious experience?

Q2 List Bandura's four stages of observational learning.

Q3 Suggest three ways a coach/teacher could make demonstrations effective.

Q4 Explain why the cognitive approach to learning may be beneficial to performers in a competitive situation.

ANSWERS

A1 Watching/observing others perform

A2 Attention; retention; motor production; motivation

A3 Choose from: use a high-status model; make them relevant; focus on specific cues; don't overload the learner; ensure learners can see and hear; vary speed of modelling; minimum time delay between instruction and demonstration; successful completion of skill; give time for mental practice/rehearsal

A4 As they understand the relationship between the stimulus and response, they are able to modify their actions based on the immediate situation and adapt their actions accordingly

examiner's **note** Draw an outline of Bandura's model and complete each section using a personal experience.

Motivation

Q1 .... motivation involves gaining self-satisfaction or pride from achievements, challenging yourself or just taking part for enjoyment.

Q2 .... motivation involves receiving some form of reward for participation from others.

Q3 Give two examples of a tangible reward.

Q4 Give two examples of an intangible reward.

ANSWERS

the internal mechanisms and external stimuli that arouse and direct behaviour

A1 Intrinsic/internal

A2 Extrinsic/external

A3 Choose from: cup; medal; certificate; money

A4 Choose from: praise; fame; recognition; records; approval from others

***examiner's* note** As well as knowing the terms, make sure you can discuss the advantages and disadvantages of each type of motivation. The use of extrinsic motivation must be monitored carefully. If it is over-used, a performer may become over-reliant and expect such a reward all the time. Initially, it is better to foster strong intrinsic motivation.

Fitts and Posner's phases of learning I

Q1 Name the three phases of learning.

Q2 What is the aim of a coach during the first phase of learning? Suggest three methods that may be employed to develop this phase successfully.

Q3 How does the nature of feedback change as the performer progresses through the various stages?

Q4 Give two ways in which a teacher can make learning during the cognitive phase easier for the performer.

ANSWERS

three progressive stages a performer experiences when learning a new skill

A1 Cognitive; associative; autonomous

A2 To create a mental picture of the task and form motor programmes; methods include demonstration, video, pictures and verbal instructions

A3 Initially, mainly extrinsic feedback from the coach; gradually the performer develops awareness of the requirements and is able to correct some of his/her own faults but still requires extrinsic feedback; finally, the performer can identify his/her own mistakes and correct most of them via intrinsic feedback

A4 Direct attention to key points; use appropriate level of language; don't overload with too much information; give time for trial and error; use adapted equipment; provide good demonstrations

***examiner's* note** You should learn the characteristics of each phase, including the use of feedback.

Fitts and Posner's phases of learning II

Q1 Outline the characteristics of the associative phase of learning.

Q2 When would you consider a performer to have reached the autonomous phase of learning?

Q3 Suggest two factors that may inhibit the performer reaching the autonomous phase.

Q4 Which phase is usually the quickest?

ANSWERS

three progressive stages a performer experiences when learning a new skill

A1 Practice phase; lots of errors and corrections; detection of gross motor errors; gradual refining of movement; change from extrinsic to intrinsic feedback; more detailed feedback provided from the coach

A2 Appears highly skilled; detects and corrects own errors; skill appears habitual; skills can be adapted to various situations; can focus on other cues; able to develop more complex skills

A3 Choose from: own ability level; motivation; complexity of task; type of practice; quality of feedback; availability of resources

A4 Cognitive

***examiner's* note** You should be able to link these phases and feedback to the cause and avoidance of plateaus.

Performance curve or graph I

Q1 A .... accelerated curve indicates a large improvement initially with only minor improvements in the later stages.

Q2 What does a linear line suggest about the performance?

Q3 Outline the type of information you might record on the *x*-axis and *y*-axis respectively.

Q4 What is a plateau?

ANSWERS

a visual representation of the performance of an individual over a period of time

A1 Negatively

A2 Gradual improvements in performance in proportion to the number of attempts or time taken

A3 *x*-axis: trials/attempts/time taken

y-axis: performance or achievement

A4 A period of time in which no significant improvement occurs in the performance

***examiner's* note** When asked to interpret a graph, you should explain what is happening to the performance over time and suggest reasons.

Performance curve or graph II

Q1 A .... accelerated curve indicates minor improvement initially but larger improvements in the later stages.

Q2 Give three possible causes of a plateau.

Q3 What is an 'ogive' or 'S-shaped' performance curve?

Q4 Suggest why plateaus should be avoided or kept to a minimum.

ANSWERS

a visual representation of the performance of an individual over a period of time

A1 Positively

A2 Choose from: complexity of the task; fatigue; lack of motivation; injury; lack of ability; boredom; limited coaching knowledge; unrealistic targets/goals; consolidation of skills; lack of understanding of the concept of plateaus and why there may be no significant improvement in performance

A3 A combination of positive, linear and negative performance curves

A4 The lack of progress can be de-motivating for the performer

***examiner's* note** When asked to 'plot' a graph, you should draw accurately; the term 'sketch' means it can be done freehand. Remember to label the axes correctly and provide a title.

Thorndike's laws of learning

Q1 Which conditioning theory is enhanced by the use of Thorndike's laws?

Q2 Explain the law of readiness.

Q3 Explain the law of exercise.

Q4 Explain the law of effect.

ANSWERS

three laws that, if applied, are thought to increase the likelihood of learning taking place

A1 Operant

A2 The performer must be physically and mentally capable of completing the task

A3 The performer must practise the task on a regular basis

A4 The performer is more likely to repeat the action if his/her behaviour is followed by effective reinforcement

***examiner's* note** To understand the laws, apply them to a practical situation you have experienced and use this to analyse their effectiveness.

17 ANSWERS

Information processing I

Q1 What is the display in the context of information processing?

Q2 What is the role of the sensory system during information processing?

Q3 Name, in order, the four basic stages of information processing.

Q4 What is perception?

ANSWERS

processing of relevant data to form a decision, which is then executed by the muscular system

A1 The physical environment surrounding the performer, containing the various stimuli used to make decisions

A2 To gather information from the display/environment using various receptors, allowing a decision to be made

A3 Input; decision making; output; feedback

A4 The interpretation and analysis of information gathered from the display by the sensory system

examiner's note Make sure you understand the key terms and sequences from both the Welford and Whiting models, and that you can apply each to a practical example.

Information processing II

Q1 ....ceptors provide intrinsic information about the movement and balance of the body.

Q2 What is the function of the translatory mechanism?

Q3 Outline the stimulus identification stage.

Q4 .... or .... are messages that are picked up via the sensory system.

ANSWERS

processing of relevant data to form a decision, which is then executed by the muscular system

A1 Proprio...

A2 To gather information about the present situation and compare it with past experiences in order to make a decision and initiate a response; it is also known as decision making

A3 This detects cues/stimuli needed to make a decision; it is also known as input

A4 Stimuli or cues

***examiner's* note** For each model, draw an outline and complete each section with a practical example based on your own experience.

Information processing III

Q1 ....ceptors gather information from outside the body via the eyes, ears, nose, mouth and touch.

Q2 Outline the response identification stage.

Q3 .... helps to filter irrelevant information and thus improve the efficiency of the information processing system.

Q4 What is the role of memory during information processing?

ANSWERS

processing of relevant data to form a decision, which is then executed by the muscular system

A1 Extero...

A2 After gathering information about the current situation, a decision is made about the appropriate movement to initiate; this is also known as the translatory mechanism/decision making

A3 Selective attention

A4 It allows the performer to gather relevant information, store it and compare it with previous experiences, and allows a decision to be made; the faster the retrieval of information, the quicker the performer's reaction time

***examiner's* note** You may be asked general questions about information processing models or about specific sections within an expanded model — for example, memory, decision making or output.

Information processing IV

Q1 ....ceptors pass information from within the internal organs of the body to the brain via the nervous system.

Q2 Outline the response programming stage.

Q3 Name, in order, the four main stages of the memory process used during information processing.

Q4 .... is the time between the onset of the stimulus and the initiation of the movement.

ANSWERS

processing of relevant data to form a decision, which is then executed by the muscular system

A1 Intero...

A2 After making a decision, the actions are implemented via the effector mechanism and the muscular system; this is also known as output

A3 Short-term sensory store; selective attention; short-term/ working memory; long-term memory

A4 Reaction time

***examiner's* note** Ensure you can outline practical strategies to develop the effectiveness of the information processing system. Examples include relevant forms of practice, mental rehearsal, stimulus intensity, development of physical fitness and effective feedback.

Information processing V

Q1 Put the following terms in the correct sequence: response programming; stimulus identification; response selection.

Q2 What is the role of the effector mechanism?

Q3 Suggest three ways in which the display could be modified to help the performer's speed of processing information.

Q4 What is the function of feedback during information processing?

ANSWERS

processing of relevant data to form a decision, which is then executed by the muscular system

A1 Stimulus identification; response selection; response programming

A2 To transfer the decision/motor programme to the muscular system via the motor nerves

A3 Choose from: increase intensity of the stimulus, e.g. brighter, larger, louder; alter shape; vary speed; change texture; alter pitch/tone; verbal cues; restrict options — reduce either stimuli or number of responses

A4 It allows errors to be identified and corrected in order to improve future performance; feedback may be obtained internally or externally

***examiner's* note** When discussing the role of feedback, use appropriate terms, such as internal, external, knowledge of result and knowledge of performance.

Decision making I

Q1 What is movement time?

Q2 What is simple reaction time?

Q3 The delay caused by an increase in information processing time when the initial stimulus is closely followed by a second stimulus is known as the ....

Q4 Suggest two factors that may affect the performer's decision-making process.

ANSWERS

a process that involves the performer combining information in order to initiate a response

A1 The time taken between the start of the movement and its completion; it does not involve reaction time

A2 The time taken to respond when presented with one stimulus and one possible response

A3 Psychological refractory period

A4 Choose from: nature of the task; individual's experience; individual's skill level; type and intensity of the stimulus

***examiner's* note** Make sure that you are able to explain the various terms, outline the relationships between them and apply each of them to a specific practical example.

Decision making II

Q1 The decision-making process is also known as the .... mechanism.

Q2 What is reaction time?

Q3 Give three forms of stimulus a performer may receive that may initiate decision making.

Q4 What is the display in the context of decision making?

ANSWERS

a process that involves the performer combining information in order to initiate a response

A1 Translatory

A2 The time between the onset of the stimulus and the initiation of movement

A3 Choose from: visual; audio; touch; kinaesthetic

A4 The physical environment surrounding the performer which contains numerous stimuli/cues

***examiner's* note** Develop an understanding of the limiting factors that can affect decision making, for example: age, intensity of stimulus, previous experience and effectiveness of selective attention capabilities.

Decision making III

Q1 What is choice reaction time?

Q2 Explain Hicks's law.

Q3 Outline the single-channel hypothesis.

Q4 The time taken from the onset of the stimulus to the completion of the movement is known as the .... time.

ANSWERS

a process that involves the performer combining information in order to initiate a response

A1 The time taken to respond when presented with a variety of stimuli, each requiring a different response

A2 The reaction time of the performer increases in proportion to the number of options available, i.e. the decision-making process takes longer if there are more possibilities available

A3 Only one piece of information can be processed by the brain at a time; the first stimulus must be cleared before the next can be processed, thus slowing reaction time

A4 Response

***examiner's* note** Practise drawing relevant diagrams, especially those relating to Hicks's law, the single-channel hypothesis and the psychological refractory period.

Decision making IV

Q1 What is stimulus–response compatibility? Suggest how it affects decision making.

Q2 .... relies on previous experience, allowing the performer to process information and initiate movement before the event actually happens.

Q3 How might the intensity of the stimulus affect reaction time?

Q4 Suggest two methods to improve reaction time and decision making.

ANSWERS

a process that involves the performer combining information in order to initiate a response

A1 The degree to which the response to a specific stimulus appears 'natural'; if the stimulus has been experienced before and the response is familiar, the reaction time will be faster

A2 Anticipation

A3 The greater the intensity, the faster the reaction time

A4 Choose from: improve selective attention; alter intensity of stimulus; improve physical fitness; anticipation; practise to recognise cues; mental rehearsal; concentrate on specific cues

***examiner's* note** You need to be able to discuss the positive and negative effects anticipation can have on performance.

Memory I

Q1 Place the following terms in the correct sequence for when a decision has to be made involving memory: long-term memory; short-term memory; short-term sensory store; selective attention

Q2 State another term often used for short-term memory.

Q3 Outline the capacity and duration of long-term memory.

Q4 What is the function of the short-term sensory store?

ANSWERS

the encoding, storage and retrieval of experience, allowing decision making to occur

A1 Short-term sensory store; selective attention; short-term memory; long-term memory

A2 Working memory or work space

A3 Capacity: unlimited

Duration: stores information indefinitely — we just have to try to retrieve it

A4 Receives information from the environment, based on which decisions can be made

***examiner's* note** You need to know the characteristics of, and relationship between, the different components of memory and be able to relate them to practical examples.

Memory II

Q1 Explain the relationship between the working memory and the long-term memory.

Q2 Outline the capacity and duration of short-term memory.

Q3 What is 'chunking' when referring to memory?

Q4 Outline the capacity and duration of the short-term sensory store.

ANSWERS

the encoding, storage and retrieval of experience, allowing decision making to occur

A1 Information must be passed from the short-term/working memory to the long-term memory for a retrieval process to occur and allow a decision to be made on the appropriate action to take; this information is compared with previous experience and a message returned to the short-term memory for execution

A2 Capacity: commonly regarded as 5–9 pieces/chunks of information

Duration: approximately 30 seconds

A3 A technique to increase the capacity of the short-term memory; pieces of information are combined together to count as one chunk

A4 Capacity: virtually limitless
Duration: less than 1 second

***examiner's* note** You should be able to outline methods of improving memory.

Memory III

Q1 What term is given to the filtering process used during information processing?

Q2 Name two factors that may affect the performer's selective attention.

Q3 How might imagery help the memory process?

Q4 Suggest three methods to improve the memory of a performer.

ANSWERS

the encoding, storage and retrieval of experience, allowing decision making to occur

A1 Selective attention

A2 Choose from: intensity of the stimulus; experience; arousal levels; quality of instruction

A3 The performer rehearses the skill and situation in his/her mind; therefore, the retrieval process from the long-term memory is faster and the appropriate message is returned quickly to the short-term memory

A4 Choose from: relevant practice; mental rehearsal; use verbal/visual guidance; chunking; increase intensity of stimulus; improve selective attention; make information relevant/fun

***examiner's* note** It may be useful to practise drawing the memory model, including the appropriate number and direction of arrows.

Motor programme I

Q1 What is a subroutine?

Q2 Suggest how the high-jump event may be divided into subroutines.

Q3 What does open-loop control mean when discussing motor control?

Q4 Outline the main difference between open-loop and closed-loop control of motor programmes.

ANSWERS

a series of movements, stored in the memory, which combine to perform a specific action

A1 A phase of a movement pattern which must be completed at the correct time in a sequence to complete the skill successfully

A2 Run-up; take-off; flight; landing

A3 The movement takes place without conscious thought and feedback because it is well learnt through repeated practice

A4 Open-loop: no feedback

Closed-loop: feedback used to modify and update movement

***examiner's* note** Make sure you can explain the difference between each form of control and the stages of the closed-loop model, with reference to a practical example.

Motor programme II

Q1 What is the role of feedback during open-loop control?

Q2 What is the function of the memory trace during closed-loop control?

Q3 What is the function of the perceptual trace during closed-loop control?

Q4 Why is feedback important during closed-loop control?

ANSWERS

a series of movements, stored in the memory, which combine to perform a specific action

A1 None — there is no feedback during open-loop control

A2 It selects and initiates movement, but does not control it

A3 It allows comparison and modification of movements, based on stored motor programmes in the long-term memory

A4 It detects errors during performance, allowing adjustments to be made; after completion of the skill, it allows comparison of performance with the current stored model, making relevant adjustments for future reference

***examiner's* note** Make sure you can explain the limitations of the motor programme model.

Schema theory I

Q1 .... schema are responsible for starting the movement.

Q2 .... schema are responsible for controlling and evaluating the movement.

Q3 Give two examples of schemas a performer may store and adapt.

Q4 Explain why practice should be varied to develop strong schemas.

ANSWERS

the idea that we store general movement patterns that are modified to adapt to the current situation

A1 Recall

A2 Recognition

A3 Choose from: running; jumping; catching; throwing; balancing

A4 Variation enables performers to experience different movement requirements, which allows them to choose the correct option as quickly as possible when confronted with a new situation

***examiner's* note** Make sure you can explain the different types of schema and sources of information used to control motor programmes and link them to specific practical examples.

Schema theory II

Q1 What are initial conditions when referring to recall schemas?

Q2 What are response specifications when referring to recall schemas?

Q3 What are sensory consequences when referring to recognition schemas?

Q4 What are response outcomes when referring to recognition schemas?

ANSWERS

the idea that we store general movement patterns that are modified to adapt to the current situation

A1 Information about the current situation, which allows a decision to be made, e.g. the position of the performer and others or the speed and direction of a ball

A2 Information about the task to be completed and formulation of a motor programme

A3 Information about feelings, during and after the movement, which allow the memory to be updated

A4 Comparisons made between the actual outcome and the intended result

***examiner's* note** You should be able to relate sources of information to practical examples.

Schema theory III

Q1 Suggest three ways in which a coach may develop strong schemas.

Q2 What is a parameter within a schema?

Q3 Explain how the schema theory overcame the limitations of the closed-loop theory of motor control.

Q4 The schema theory supports the principle of .... of learning between skills.

ANSWERS

the idea that we store general movement patterns that are modified to adapt to the current situation

A1 Choose from: vary practice; make practice realistic; make practice relevant to the actual situation; provide quality feedback; avoid massed practice; make practice challenging and progressive

A2 Information that is stored within a schema, which allows the performer to choose the correct speed and force required depending on the current situation

A3 Not all motor programmes have to be stored in the memory; explains how complex, quick movements are executed; explains how motor programmes can be formed for new situations without practice

A4 Transfer

***examiner's* note** Don't confuse schema theory with transfer of learning.

Feedback I

Q1 Suggest two reasons why feedback is used.

Q2 .... feedback is received via the proprioceptors, developing a performer's kinaesthetic awareness.

Q3 What is the term for feedback given after the activity?

Q4 What is knowledge of results in the context of feedback?

ANSWERS

information received either during or after completion of the performance

A1 Choose from: to correct faults; to provide motivation; to reinforce actions

A2 Intrinsic/internal

A3 Terminal feedback

A4 Information received about the outcome or result of the action, e.g. finishing position in a race, time, distance recorded, goals scored, percentage figures for completed skills

***examiner's* note** You should be able to outline each term and discuss how to optimise the use of feedback.

Feedback II

Q1 What is extrinsic feedback? Give two examples of how a performer may receive this form of feedback.

Q2 Why is continuous feedback useful to a performer?

Q3 How does knowledge of performance differ from knowledge of results?

Q4 Suggest two ways in which the coach can make the use of feedback more effective.

ANSWERS

information received either during or after completion of the performance

A1 Feedback received from an external source, e.g. from a coach/teacher, spectators or team-mates

A2 As the information is received during the performance, modifications can be made immediately rather than waiting until the end

A3 Knowledge of performance is about technique and/or execution of tactics; knowledge of results is about outcome and end result

A4 Choose from: give immediately if possible; don't overload the performer with too much information; ensure the performer does not become dependent on feedback; combine visual and verbal feedback; allow time for the performer to evaluate feedback

***examiner's* note** You should be able to relate the use of feedback to the various stages of learning.

Transfer of learning I

Q1 .... transfer occurs when a skill currently being learned has an effect on a skill in the future.

Q2 What is bilateral transfer? Give an example to illustrate your answer.

Q3 What is positive transfer of learning?

Q4 Suggest two ways in which a coach could ensure that positive transfer occurs.

ANSWERS

the effect that the learning of one skill has on the learning of another skill

A1 Proactive

A2 Transfer of learning that occurs from one limb to another, rather than from task to task, e.g. dribbling the ball with the right hand in basketball helps the development of left-handed dribbling

A3 When skills that are previously learned aid the learning of new skills

A4 Choose from: make practice similar to a game; ensure the original skill is well learned before progressing; explain the concept of transfer to the performer; develop skills in a closed situation first; make the movement and cognitive requirements of the skill similar

***examiner's* note** Make sure you can explain each term and give specific examples to illustrate your understanding.

Transfer of learning II

Q1 .... transfer occurs when a previously learned skill hinders the development of a new skill.

Q2 What is retroactive transfer?

Q3 Explain the term 'zero transfer'.

Q4 What is the difference between near and far transfer?

ANSWERS

the effect that the learning of one skill has on the learning of another skill

A1 Negative

A2 Transfer of learning when the skill currently being learned has an effect on one that was developed previously

A3 The learning of one skill might have no effect on another

A4 In near transfer the performer completes skills practices that are similar to the actual game situation; in far transfer the performer completes skills that are general in nature and may be used later to transfer to other, more specific situations

***examiner's* note** The effective use of knowledge of transfer can improve the performer's skill level by reducing the amount of practice needed to improve on specific weaknesses.

Guidance I

Q1 What form of guidance is most effective to help the performer create a mental picture of the action?

Q2 What is manual guidance?

Q3 What form of guidance involves the performer being told what to do?

Q4 What is mechanical guidance? Give an example.

ANSWERS

information provided by the coach or teacher to aid the learning of skills

A1 Visual

A2 This involves the performer being physically placed/supported in or forced into the correct position

A3 Verbal

A4 This involves the performer being supported by some form of device, e.g. a harness or a swimming float

***examiner's* note** Make sure you are able to give examples of each form of guidance and the situations in which they are most useful.

Guidance II

Q1 Give three examples of how a coach may use visual guidance.

Q2 Suggest two advantages of mechanical and manual guidance.

Q3 Which form of guidance is probably the most useful during the cognitive and associative stages of learning?

Q4 Suggest two ways to maximise the effect of verbal guidance.

ANSWERS

information provided by the coach or teacher to aid the learning of skills

A1 Choose from: demonstration; video; photos; diagrams; chalk marks, hoops and cones

A2 Choose from: safe in dangerous situations; develop confidence; develop kinaesthetic awareness; restrict movements and so force the performer into the correct position

A3 Visual

A4 Choose from: don't overload the performer with information; use an appropriate level of language; highlight key points to focus attention; allow the performer time to evaluate the comments; combine with visual guidance to clarify understanding

***examiner's* note** Make sure you can list advantages and disadvantages of each form of guidance.

Teaching styles I

Q1 Suggest three factors that need to be considered before deciding on the most appropriate teaching style.

Q2 Explain what is meant by the command style of teaching.

Q3 Which style involves the teacher setting a task that the learners have to complete in pairs, alternating roles as observer and performer?

Q4 How would a teacher use the discovery style of teaching?

ANSWERS

a continuum reflecting the degree to which decisions are made by the teacher and/or student

A1 Choose from: nature of the situation; ability of the performer; personality of the teacher; experience of the teacher; nature of the task; time available

A2 The teacher is autocratic, making all the decisions, with no input from the group

A3 Reciprocal style

A4 Set a task and provide clues; ask appropriate questions at key times; make suggestions

***examiner's* note** Make sure you can name and give characteristics of each style and the situations in which they are most useful.

Teaching styles II

Q1 Give two advantages of the command style of teaching and suggest two situations where its use can be effective.

Q2 Give two disadvantages of the reciprocal style of teaching.

Q3 Which style is most appropriate when instructing a group abseiling for the first time?

Q4 Explain the problem-solving style of teaching.

ANSWERS

a continuum reflecting the degree to which decisions are made by the teacher and/or student

A1 Advantages — choose from: gives clear objectives; maintains control; good for outlining safety procedures

Situations — choose from: large groups; dangerous situations; limited time available; working with novices

A2 Choose from: difficult to monitor all pairs; learning takes place at different rates; poor technique and understanding may develop

A3 Command style

A4 Learners are set a task and have to find their own solution; it is often linked to the discovery/guided-discovery style

***examiner's* note** Make sure you can list the advantages and disadvantages of each style of teaching.

Teaching styles III

Q1 Which style is most appropriate when teaching a PE lesson to a group of Year 9 students who are devising a gymnastics routine?

Q2 Give two advantages of the discovery style of teaching.

Q3 Give two disadvantages of the command style of teaching.

Q4 Give two advantages of the reciprocal style of teaching.

ANSWERS

a continuum reflecting the degree to which decisions are made by the teacher and/or student

A1 Problem solving or guided discovery

A2 Choose from: greater understanding of the task for the learner; allows for creativity; develops decision-making skills; greater self-satisfaction and motivation

A3 Choose from: no input from the learner, causing poor motivation; difficult to provide individual feedback; little social interaction within the group; little creativity and decision making

A4 Choose from: more pupil decision making; pupils learn at their own rate; development of analysis skills; more social interaction; greater understanding of movement; development of communication skills

***examiner's* note** You need to be able to explain the variables affecting the choice of style — teacher, activity, learner and situation.

Teaching styles IV

Q1 Why might the discovery style be inadvisable in some situations?

Q2 Which is the most appropriate style of teaching when developing the basketball lay-up skill with a group of Year 11 GCSE students?

Q3 Suggest two advantages of the problem-solving approach.

Q4 Why should a variety of teaching styles be used?

ANSWERS

a continuum reflecting the degree to which decisions are made by the teacher and/or student

A1 Time might be limited; individuals learn at different rates; it may be hard to monitor everyone's progress; safety issues may be an important factor; learners may not have the experience to complete the task

A2 Reciprocal

A3 Choose from: gives the learner responsibility; develops creativity; maintains motivation; develops social interaction/ communication skills; develops understanding via trial and error; individuals progress at their own rate

A4 To cater for the changing needs of the learner and the situation; to maintain motivation and clarify understanding

***examiner's* note** Use a diagram to clarify the teaching style continuum.

Presentation of practice I

Q1 What is the whole approach method of practice?

Q2 The .... method involves the performer attempting to develop specific subroutines of a skill in isolation before putting them into the correct sequence.

Q3 Which approach does the term 'chaining' refer to?

Q4 Why might the whole–part–whole approach be advantageous to a long jumper in the associative phase of learning?

ANSWERS

the structuring of practice into phases or subroutines, depending on the nature of the skill

A1 The performer attempts to complete the entire movement, after observing a demonstration of the skill or being given verbal instructions

A2 Part approach

A3 Progressive part approach

A4 It promotes awareness of the overall feeling of the movement but can then develop specific phases, e.g. take-off and flight, before an attempt to reintroduce them to the complete action

***examiner's* note** Make sure you can list the advantages and disadvantages of each form of presentation of practice.

Presentation of practice II

Q1 When would the part-approach method of presentation be beneficial in terms of the performer and the task?

Q2 Give two advantages of the whole approach method of presentation.

Q3 The ....–..................–.................. approach involves gaining experience of the complete skill before refining specific subroutines.

Q4 When would the whole approach method of presentation be beneficial in terms of the performer and the task?

ANSWERS

the structuring of practice into phases or subroutines, depending on the nature of the skill

A1 Performer: novice; limited attention span; limited motivation; requires attention to a particular subroutine; using massed practice

Task: sequences/serial skills; complex skills; dangerous skills

A2 Choose from: develops a kinaesthetic feel for the complete action; good for skills that are difficult to break down; less time-consuming

A3 Whole–part–whole

A4
- When the performer is motivated, experienced and has high levels of attention, while the task is simple, discrete, ballistic in nature and difficult to break down
- When the performer is a novice and the task is modified/simplified to allow him/her to gain an awareness of the overall movement

***examiner's* note** Effective practice should not only improve performance, but also maintain motivation.

Presentation of practice III

Q1 Explain why the skill of hurdling would lend itself to the part approach method of practice.

Q2 Give two advantages of using the progressive part approach.

Q3 Give one disadvantage of using the progressive part approach.

Q4 Why should a coach be flexible in his/her method of presentation?

ANSWERS

the structuring of practice into phases or subroutines, depending on the nature of the skill

A1 The overall skill can be broken down and taught in discrete elements, allowing the performer to experience each before combining them into the whole action

A2 Choose from: helps develop a complex task; useful for those with limited attention span; coordination of temporal and spatial components can be experienced; aids transfer to whole practice

A3 Choose from: time-consuming; lack of awareness of overall action; can be de-motivating if not completing full movement/ sequence

A4 Each situation may require a different approach to obtain the optimum result; a combination of all approaches may be the best option

***examiner's* note** Often a teacher/coach may use a combination of styles, depending on the nature of the skill and the performer.

Types of practice I

Q1 Suggest three factors a coach should consider when deciding which form of practice would be most suitable.

Q2 What is massed practice?

Q3 .... practice involves the performer completing a set of tasks, then taking a recovery period before progressing to the next set of tasks.

Q4 What is mental practice?

ANSWERS

different approaches to practice at allocated times that let performers reinforce, develop and refine learning

A1 Choose from: size and structure of the group; ability of the performer(s); motivation of the performer(s); nature/complexity of the task; facilities; time available

A2 Continuous practice with little or no recovery between sets or trials

A3 Distributed

A4 This involves the cognitive or mental rehearsal of a skill without physical movement; the performer imagines completing the action successfully, developing and recreating the kinaesthetic feeling of the movement

***examiner's* note** Make sure you can outline different types of practice and cite examples of when each method would be the most appropriate.

Types of practice II

Q1 Suggest three ways in which the recovery period during distributed practice can be used effectively.

Q2 Explain three ways in which mental practice can help the performer.

Q3 What is variable practice?

Q4 Outline when the use of massed practice would be advisable and beneficial in terms of the performer and the task.

ANSWERS

different approaches to practice at allocated times that let performers reinforce, develop and refine learning

A1 Choose from: to reduce fatigue; for mental practice; to provide feedback; to provide alternative activity; to refocus and motivate the performer

A2 Choose from: it can raise motivation/confidence by only seeing success; recreate the kinaesthetic feel of good actions; control arousal levels; evaluate feedback; focus attention; reduce reaction time and improve anticipation

A3 A form of practice involving a combination of massed and distributed practice, possibly including both open and closed skills

A4 Performer: experienced; well motivated; good fitness levels

Task: discrete; simple

examiner's note Make sure you can list advantages and disadvantages of each type of practice.

Types of practice III

Q1 How can a performer maximise the use of mental practice?

Q2 Outline when the use of distributed practice would be advisable and beneficial in terms of the performer and the task.

Q3 Give two disadvantages of using massed practice.

Q4 Which type of practice would be the most appropriate for a professional tennis player who needs to refine his serve-and-volley technique before a tournament? Why?

ANSWERS

different approaches to practice at allocated times that let performers reinforce, develop and refine learning

A1 Imagine only success — avoid failure; develop clear images; sequence the action; practice in a quiet place; practice on a regular basis

A2 Performer: novice/less experienced; less well motivated, limited fitness level

Task: gross skills; complex skills; continuous; dangerous

A3 Choose from: boredom; fatigue; loss of concentration; lack of variety

A4 Massed practice, as he is skilled, motivated, has high levels of fitness and is completing a discrete skill

examiner's note Develop an understanding of how the effective use of practice can influence motivation, and vice versa.

Personality: trait theory

Q1 What is a trait?

Q2 Outline the differences between an extrovert and an introvert personality.

Q3 What does the trait theory suggest about choice of sporting activity?

Q4 Explain the difference between type A and type B personalities.

ANSWERS

the idea that more-or-less stable, enduring, unique characteristics determine behaviour

A1 An innate, enduring characteristic possessed by an individual that can be used to explain and predict his/her behaviour in different situations

A2 An extrovert is sociable, outgoing, active, optimistic and impulsive; an introvert is quiet, unsociable, passive, careful and reserved

A3 Extroverts are more likely to play team sports and introverts individual sports

A4 Type A personalities experience high levels of stress, have a strong competitive drive, find it hard to delegate, and need to be in control of the situation; type B personalities are more relaxed, less competitive, experience lower levels of stress, and delegate easily

***examiner's* note** Make sure you can outline the various personality theories and evaluate their strengths and weaknesses.

Personality: interactionist theory I

Q1 The interactionist theory proposes that specific personality types are suited to particular sports. True or false?

Q2 What are the characteristics of the deep psychological core, as suggested by Hollander?

Q3 What does Hollander suggest influences the outer layer of his model, the role-related behaviour?

Q4 Trait theories are good predictors of sporting success. True or false?

ANSWERS

the idea that personality is due to a combination of innate traits and interaction with the environment

A1 False

A2 The characteristics are generally stable and are the primary influences on behaviour. They include self-concept, perceived ability, attitudes and achievement orientation

A3 The specific situation, which may cause the personality and behaviour of a performer to alter

A4 False

***examiner's* note** Learn the characteristics of different types of personality and be able to outline suitable roles for each type. You will be required to evaluate the effectiveness of each theory with reference to success in sport and elite performance.

Personality: interactionist theory II

Q1 Explain the formula $B = f(PE)$.

Q2 How does the interactionist theory differ from the trait theory?

Q3 How can coaches use the knowledge gained from observing particular behaviour patterns?

Q4 Name the three interrelated layers, as suggested by Hollander.

ANSWERS

the idea that personality is due to a combination of innate traits and interaction with the environment

A1 Behaviour (*B*) is a function (f) of personality traits (*P*) and the environment (*E*)

A2 It explains why some performers react differently in different situations, i.e. their personality alters to suit the requirements of the situation, rather than behaving in the same manner in all situations

A3 Strengths and weaknesses can be identified and appropriate strategies implemented to modify the actions of a performer as required

A4 Deep psychological core; typical responses; role-related behaviour

***examiner's* note** Be able to compare the different theories of personality and evaluate each one.

Personality testing I

Q1 Name the three most common methods used to measure personality.

Q2 What does the term 'reliability' mean with reference to testing?

Q3 Outline Eysenck's personality inventory (EPI).

Q4 Suggest two advantages of using self-report questionnaires.

ANSWERS

a range of methods used to assess the characteristics of an individual

A1 Self-report questionnaires; observation; interviews

A2 The test can be repeated to produce similar results

A3 A series of questions with 'yes' or 'no' responses used to measure levels of introversion/extroversion and stable/neurotic dimensions

A4 Choose from: quick to use; specific questions can be asked; confidential; a large amount of data can be collected at one time

***examiner's* note** Make sure you understand and can explain the terms 'validity' and 'reliability' when discussing methods.

Personality testing II

Q1 Outline the sports competition anxiety test (SCAT).

Q2 Explain the term 'validity' with reference to testing procedures.

Q3 Suggest two disadvantages of the observational method of data collection.

Q4 Name the two forms of anxiety measured by the CSAI-2 test.

ANSWERS

a range of methods used to assess the characteristics of an individual

A1 A self-report questionnaire, completed prior to competition. It measures competitive trait anxiety, which can be used to help predict levels of anxiety in a specific situation

A2 The ability of a test to produce accurate results. A test with internal validity produces required data with all possible variables kept to a minimum; in a test with external validity, the data can be applied to a wider population

A3 Choose from: time-consuming; subjective; need to know the behaviour patterns of the performer; raises concerns about validity

A4 Cognitive-state anxiety and somatic-state anxiety

***examiner's* note** Make sure you can outline the most commonly used tests and critically evaluate their use.

Profile of mood states (POMS)

Q1 The POMS for a performer with positive mental health is commonly known as the i.................. p...................

Q2 Name three mood states measured by the POMS questionnaire.

Q3 All successful elite athletes display a positive profile. True or false?

Q4 Which mood state gives the graph a distinctive peak?

ANSWERS

a questionnaire aiming to equate positive mental health with success in sport

A1 Iceberg profile

A2 Choose from: tension; depression; anger; vigour; fatigue; confusion

A3 False

A4 Vigour

***examiner's* note** You need to understand the relationship between successful performers and POMS, but also the limitations of the theory. It is unlikely that you will be asked to draw a graph, but you will have to be able to interpret one and explain the shape of the iceberg profile.

Achievement motivation theory I

Q1 Name the two factors that influence a performer's achievement motivation.

Q2 What are the two types of personality suggested by Atkinson's achievement motivation theory?

Q3 Name the two aspects that are evaluated when referring to the 'situation' that might affect the performer's motivation.

Q4 Achievement goals can be 'outcome-oriented'. What does this mean?

ANSWERS

behaviour is based on interaction with the environment and desire to succeed

A1 Personality factors and situational factors

A2 'Need to achieve' (Nach) and 'need to avoid failure' (Naf)

A3 Probability of success and incentive value

A4 Goals are based on the end result or on comparison with others

***examiner's* note** You should be able to explain, with the aid of practical examples, how the different types of personality will approach a specific situation. Different types will tend either to be positive and take on the challenge or to worry about failure and choose the easy option.

Achievement motivation theory II

Q1 Give three characteristics of a Nach performer.

Q2 Give three characteristics of a Naf performer.

Q3 Achievement goals can be 'task-oriented'. What does this mean?

Q4 Performers with a Naf personality tend to choose tasks that are either very easy or very difficult. True or false?

ANSWERS

behaviour is based on interaction with the environment and desire to succeed

A1 Choose from: likes challenges; likes feedback; takes responsibility for own actions; persistent; confident; completes task quickly; optimistic; task goal oriented

A2 Choose from: gives up easily; avoids challenges; pessimistic; takes time over the task; avoids personal responsibility; avoids 50:50 situations; does not like feedback; outcome oriented

A3 Goals are used to judge the performance of an individual against his/her own standards rather than those of others

A4 True

***examiner's* note** Learn the characteristics of each personality type and how these might influence the type of goal setting that is used.

Achievement motivation theory III

Q1 Suggest two strategies a coach could use to improve the Nach characteristics of a performer.

Q2 Suggest a criticism of the achievement motivation theory.

Q3 Name Veroff's three stages of achievement motivation.

Q4 Suggest why it is important to develop Nach performers.

ANSWERS

behaviour is based on interaction with the environment and desire to succeed

A1 Choose from: positive experiences; use attributions correctly; set realistic goals; establish a non-evaluative environment; reinforcement from significant others; develop high levels of self-efficacy

A2 Choose from: too simplistic; performers may perceive success and failure in different ways; incentive values may vary

A3 Autonomous competence; social comparison; integrated

A4 Prepared to improve their performance; highly motivated; effective in group situations; have pride in their performance; will continue with task; develop approach behaviour

***examiner's* note** You need to be able to outline the different types of goals that can be used, with practical examples, and say which is most appropriate for each type of personality.

Attitude I

Q1 What is an attitude object?

Q2 Name two common forms of questionnaire used to measure the attitude of an individual.

Q3 Attitudes can be used to predict behaviour. True or false?

Q4 List the three components of the triadic model.

ANSWERS

a relatively stable belief or view

A1 The focus of an individual's attitude, e.g. a person, an item, an idea or an event

A2 Choose from: Likert scale; Thurston scale; Osgood scale

A3 False

A4 Cognitive; affective; behavioural

***examiner's* note** Make sure you can explain how an attitude is formed, its components, methods of measuring attitude, implications for the coach and ways of altering negative attitude.

Attitude II

Q1 Give three factors that might influence the formation of an attitude.

Q2 Explain the cognitive component of a person's attitude.

Q3 Explain the affective component of a person's attitude.

Q4 Explain the behavioural component of a person's attitude.

ANSWERS

a relatively stable belief or view

A1 Choose from: past experience; parents and family; peer group; role models; socialisation; media; familiarity; conditioning

A2 Thoughts and beliefs about the attitude object

A3 Emotions and feelings towards the attitude object

A4 Actions towards the attitude object

***examiner's* note** Make sure you can explain each component of the triadic model and give specific examples of how each may be altered.

Attitude III

Q1 What is a stereotype?

Q2 What is prejudice?

Q3 Name the three most common methods used to measure a person's attitude.

Q4 Measuring a person's attitude is usually reliable and valid. True or false?

ANSWERS

a relatively stable belief or view

A1 An overly simplistic image shared by all members of a social group; stereotypes are usually negative and can affect the attitude and behaviour of an individual

A2 An extreme attitude, usually unfavourable, often based on inadequate or inaccurate facts and leading to intolerance or dislike of people from a certain race, religion or culture

A3 Observation of behaviour; physiological tests; questionnaires or interviews

A4 False

***examiner's* note** Be able to explain the various methods of measuring attitude and outline the limitations and advantages of each.

Changing attitudes

Q1 Explain the cognitive dissonance theory.

Q2 Suggest three strategies to improve the attitude of a performer.

Q3 How can the effectiveness of the persuasive communication technique be maximised?

Q4 Give two reasons why a performer's attitude may need to be changed.

ANSWERS

altering the negative attitude of an individual to a positive one

A1 One component of the triadic model is altered to create feelings of psychological discomfort; the performer then questions his/her current attitude and to return to a consistent state either the new attitude is adopted or the original one is maintained

A2 Choose from: praise/rewards; goal setting; use of role models; correct use of attributions; variable practice; make activities fun; give responsibility

A3 Ensure that: the person delivering the message is of high status; the message is of good quality; the message can be delivered and understood

A4 Choose from: to break down stereotypes; to stop prejudice; to increase motivation; to alter behaviour patterns

***examiner's* note** Make sure you can apply the methods to practical situations and give relevant examples.

Aggression I

Q1 What is the difference between an aggressive act and an assertive act?

Q2 Outline the instinct theory of aggression.

Q3 Give three practical examples of possible causes of aggression during a game.

Q4 The frustration–aggression hypothesis suggests that frustration will always lead to aggression. True or false?

ANSWERS

behaviour intended to injure another person, either verbally or physically, outside the laws of the game

A1 An assertive act is within the laws of the game

A2 We are born with aggressive tendencies as part of our evolutionary inheritance, to help us survive; performers may have an instinctive reaction or wish to establish control over their territory

A3 Choose from: actions of the opponent; blocking of a specific goal; poor individual performance; performance of team-mates; crowd; referee's decisions; weather; facilities; result; pain; fear; extrinsic rewards; status of the game; expectation of others

A4 True

examiner's **note** You need to be able to give examples of aggressive and assertive acts and to justify your choices.

Aggression II

Q1 Outline two criticisms of the frustration–aggression hypothesis.

Q2 How does the aggressive cue theory differ from the frustration–aggression hypothesis?

Q3 Explain the social learning theory of aggression.

Q4 Explain how catharsis might influence aggression.

ANSWERS

behaviour intended to injure another person, either verbally or physically, outside the laws of the game

A1 Choose from: it does not account for acts of premeditated aggression; not all frustration leads to aggression; it does not allow for instinctive reactions; aggression can be a learned response

A2 It suggests that acts of aggression will only occur if a socially learnt cue is present in the environment that makes the act acceptable

A3 Aggression is a learned response; acts of aggression are observed, copied and reinforced, often by a significant other

A4 It might release the built-up stress or frustration in a player and allow him/her to return to a calmer state

examiner's note You need to be able to outline the various theories of aggression and comment on their validity.

Control of aggression

Q1 Suggest three strategies a coach might use to limit the aggressive acts committed by a player.

Q2 Outline how officials can limit aggressive acts.

Q3 Spectators often become aggressive. Suggest two strategies for reducing such aggressive behaviour.

Q4 Goal setting is an effective method of controlling aggression. True or false?

ANSWERS

methods used to reduce the over-arousal of a performer

A1 Choose from: punishment and fines; drop the player from the team; reduce emphasis on end result; substitution; reward non-aggressive behaviour; show positive and negative role models; stress management techniques; develop fitness levels

A2 Assert control from the start of the game; enforce rules correctly; be consistent; punish aggressive acts immediately

A3 Choose from: positive player role models; limits on alcohol; restricted seating areas; reducing levels of rivalry; good quality refereeing; coaches not encouraging violent acts; responsible media coverage

A4 True

***examiner's* note** Be able to give practical examples of methods of controlling aggressive players and comment on the implications they may have for the player's performance.

Reticular activating system (RAS)

Q1 What is the purpose of the RAS?

Q2 Extroverts tend to seek higher levels of arousal as their RAS lacks stimulation. True or false?

Q3 Why do introverts seek low levels of arousal?

Q4 Where is the RAS located?

ANSWERS

a cluster of brain cells that maintains levels of arousal

A1 It is a filter mechanism for information entering the brain, either allowing information to enter or inhibiting it

A2 True

A3 Their RAS is already stimulated, while the RAS of extroverts has naturally low levels of stimulation and requires additional sources of arousal to become satisfied

A4 In the central part of the brain stem

***examiner's* note** Make sure you understand the relationship between the RAS and arousal levels for different personality types.

Drive theory

Q1 Explain the formula $P = H \times D$.

Q2 What does the drive theory suggest will happen as arousal levels increase?

Q3 How will increased arousal levels affect the performance of experienced and novice performers?

Q4 What is the main criticism of the drive theory?

ANSWERS

a theory suggesting a linear relationship between arousal and performance

A1 Performance (*P*) is a result of habit (or dominant response) (*H*) and drive (*D*)

A2 The dominant learnt response of the performer is more likely to occur

A3 Experienced — performance improves; novice — performance declines

A4 It does not account for the experienced performer making mistakes when arousal levels increase

***examiner's* note** It is a common mistake for students to think that as the level of arousal increases, so does the level of performance. In reality, the dominant response is likely to occur, which may or may not be skilled.

Inverted U theory I

Q1 What are the characteristics of a performer who is under-aroused?

Q2 What are the characteristics of a performer who is over-aroused?

Q3 What is the term given to the optimal level of arousal that will produce the best performance?

Q4 Which level of arousal is said to produce the best performance?

ANSWERS

a theory proposing that performance improves with arousal levels, but only up to an optimum point

A1 Poor selective attention; lack of concentration; lack of assertive behaviour; poor coordination with team-mates; misses vital cues

A2 Aggressive behaviour; poor selective attention; attentional narrowing; poor coordination with team-mates; anxiety; errors in skill reproduction

A3 Zone of optimal functioning

A4 Moderate level

***examiner's* note** You need to understand the relationships between, and limitations of, the different theories of arousal and to be able to outline methods of controlling arousal levels.

Inverted U theory II

Q1 Skills that require fine muscle movements need a high level of arousal. True or false?

Q2 How does the skill level of a performer affect his/her optimum arousal level?

Q3 Simple skills are best performed with low levels of arousal. True or false?

Q4 Explain how the personality of a performer may influence his/her optimum level of arousal.

ANSWERS

a theory proposing that performance improves with arousal levels, but only up to an optimum point

A1 False

A2 An experienced performer is able to cope better with higher levels of arousal than a novice

A3 False

A4 Extroverts are able to cope better with higher levels of arousal than introverts

***examiner's* note** Make sure you understand that the optimum level of arousal can alter for each performer, depending on the task and the situation. Reinforce your answers with practical examples. Areas of possible variability include the personality of the performer, his/her experience and the nature of the task, in terms of complexity and gross/fine movement.

Catastrophe theory

Q1 Catastrophe theory states that performances of over-aroused individuals will always continue to deteriorate. True or false?

Q2 How does catastrophe theory differ from the inverted U theory?

Q3 The optimum point of arousal in the catastrophe theory is different from that in the inverted U theory. True or false?

Q4 How can performers recover their arousal levels and avoid catastrophe?

ANSWERS

a theory suggesting a sudden, dramatic collapse in performance at a certain arousal level

A1 False

A2 It suggests that even if performers do become over-aroused, they might be able to recover and regain their optimum level of arousal and perform effectively; the inverted U theory does not allow for a recovery in performance

A3 False

A4 Stress management techniques — cognitive and somatic; encouragement from coach; peer support

***examiner's* note** You should be able to sketch a graph of the theory and interpret its shape when linked to a practical example.

Attentional narrowing

Q1 How does over-arousal affect a performer's ability to focus on relevant cues?

Q2 What is attentional wastage?

Q3 Suggest two strategies a performer may use to maintain his/her selective attention.

Q4 How can the cue utilisation theory aid attentional narrowing?

ANSWERS

an idea that links arousal theories to the individual's ability to focus on relevant cues

A1 It hinders the process, causing important cues to be missed

A2 This occurs when the performer loses concentration and misdirects his/her focus onto irrelevant cues

A3 Choose from: block out the crowd; stress management techniques; practice during training; increase motivation levels; reach optimum levels of arousal; alter intensity of the stimulus

A4 Redirection of thoughts causes the performer to focus on important cues and block out those that are irrelevant

***examiner's* note** You need to understand the relationship between attentional narrowing and arousal theories, and to be able to explain when attentional narrowing occurs and its impact on performance.

Social facilitation I

Q1 What effect might social facilitation have on a novice performer and why?

Q2 Social facilitation is caused by 'others'. Name the four categories of others.

Q3 Suggest three strategies a coach might employ to reduce the effects of social facilitation and improve performance.

Q4 The drive theory states that the performance of extrovert performers decreases in the presence of others. True or false?

ANSWERS

the influence of the presence of others on performance

A1 Performance may decrease because (according to the drive theory) as arousal levels increase, the dominant habit is more likely to be produced; this is known as social inhibition

A2 The audience; coactors; competitive coactors; social reinforcers

A3 Choose from: use an audience in training; reduce the importance given to the event; improve selective attention; use mental rehearsal techniques; set realistic goals; use cognitive and somatic stress management techniques

A4 False; it should be enhanced by the presence of others.

***examiner's* note** Give clear explanations and examples of the different types of 'others' and be aware of strategies to reduce the effects of social facilitation if performance is deteriorating because of the presence of others.

Social facilitation II

Q1 What effect might social facilitation have on an experienced performer and why?

Q2 What are coactors?

Q3 What are competitive coactors?

Q4 What is the difference between 'primary spectators' and 'secondary spectators'?

ANSWERS

the influence of the presence of others on performance

A1 Performance may increase because (according to the drive theory) as arousal levels increase, the dominant habit is more likely to be produced

A2 Those performing the same task as the performer but not in direct competition

A3 Those in direct competition with the performer

A4 Primary spectators are those present at the event; secondary spectators are those following the event elsewhere via the media, e.g. television, radio, newspapers or the internet

***examiner's* note** Make sure you understand the relationship between drive theory and social facilitation. Don't get confused and think that performance increases with arousal — it depends on the experience of the performer.

Evaluation apprehension

Q1 How does evaluation apprehension differ from social facilitation?

Q2 What aspects of the crowd can influence evaluation apprehension?

Q3 Suggest two strategies to reduce the effects of evaluation apprehension.

Q4 'Home advantage' will always improve the performance of a player. True or false?

ANSWERS

anxiety caused by a performer's perception that he/she is being judged by the audience

A1 Social facilitation suggests that the presence of others will affect arousal levels; evaluation apprehension suggests that the presence of others will only have an effect if the performer feels his or her performance is being judged

A2 Proximity; size; knowledge; hostility; noise level

A3 Choose from: train with an audience; develop selective attention; reduce the importance given to the event; use mental rehearsal techniques; set realistic goals; use cognitive and somatic stress management techniques; encourage peer support

A4 False

***examiner's* note** Make sure that you understand the relationship between social facilitation and evaluation apprehension.

Self-efficacy I

Q1 Why is it important to develop a performer's self-efficacy?

Q2 How does self-efficacy differ from self-confidence?

Q3 Name the four factors that contribute to an individual's level of self-efficacy.

Q4 Why are performance accomplishments important in developing self-efficacy?

ANSWERS

the degree of self-confidence of a performer in a specific situation

A1 To build confidence in his/her ability to perform the skills and execute tactics effectively; he/she will be more constructive within a group, more inclined to learn new skills and less likely to exhibit social loafing

A2 Self-efficacy is situation-specific; self-confidence is general to all aspects of life

A3 Performance accomplishments; vicarious experiences; verbal persuasion; emotional and psychological arousal

A4 Experiences of success will increase motivation and confidence whereas failures will demotivate the performer

***examiner's* note** Learn the sections of the diagrammatic model of self-efficacy and apply each to practical examples.

Self-efficacy II

Q1 How can verbal persuasion influence the development of self-efficacy?

Q2 How does emotional arousal affect self-efficacy?

Q3 What are vicarious experiences?

Q4 Suggest two methods of developing self-efficacy.

ANSWERS

the degree of self-confidence of a performer in a specific situation

A1 Encouragement from others, particularly significant others, allows performers to feel more confident about their abilities and actions, leading them to continue to develop their skills

A2 The level of arousal a performer naturally experiences can be viewed negatively (e.g. sweating, increased heart rate), but it should be seen as a readiness to perform and a positive factor

A3 Experiences that involve watching others complete the task

A4 Choose from: positive experiences with success; observation of others (especially of a similar standard); encouragement; positive feedback; stress management techniques; goal setting

***examiner's* note** Develop knowledge of how to improve the self-efficacy of a performer and use specific examples to highlight your understanding.

Vealey's sport-specific model of sport confidence

Q1 What does Vealey mean by 'sport confidence'?

Q2 Explain the term 'trait sport confidence'.

Q3 Explain the term 'state sport confidence'.

Q4 What other factor combines with SC-trait influencing the performer's SC-state?

ANSWERS

trait confidence and competitive orientation both influence and are influenced by subjective outcomes

A1 The belief or degree of certainty that individuals possess about their ability to be successful in sport

A2 The stable characteristics of an individual's personality that are relevant in all sporting situations; some performers may appear confident in all situations

A3 The level of self-confidence experienced in a specific sporting situation; this is a key factor affecting the overall level of self-confidence

A4 Objective sport situation and competitive orientation (type of goals set, either performance-oriented or outcome-oriented)

***examiner's* note** You may be required to outline the components of Vealey's model and explain the relationship between each. Ensure you can describe how the outcome may affect future participation and levels of self-efficacy.

Attribution theory I

Q1 Give two examples of an internal stable factor.

Q2 Give two examples of an internal unstable factor.

Q3 Give two examples of an external stable factor.

Q4 Give two examples of an external unstable factor.

ANSWERS

the idea that the reasons perceived by a performer for the outcome of his/her actions can affect motivation

A1 Choose from: ability; skills; fitness levels

A2 Choose from: effort; arousal levels; practice; motivation

A3 Coaching; quality of the opposition

A4 Choose from: officials; luck; weather; facilities; teamwork

***examiner's* note** You should be able to draw or interpret a diagram of Weiner's model and annotate it. You might be presented with different scenarios, so practise giving appropriate attributions, with examples. Look at elite sports performers, coaches and managers, and identify the reasons they give for different performance outcomes.

Attribution theory II

Q1 Why is it important to use attributions correctly?

Q2 Failure should be attributed to internal stable factors. True or false?

Q3 What is self-serving bias?

Q4 List the four categories of causal attributions.

ANSWERS

the idea that the reasons perceived by a performer for the outcome of his/her actions can affect motivation

A1 To maintain motivation; develop high self-efficacy; avoid learned helplessness; encourage performers to continue with activity; influence emotional feelings

A2 False

A3 The tendency of performers to attribute success to internal factors and failure to external factors, which allows them to protect their self-esteem and maintain levels of motivation

A4 Ability; effort; task difficulty; luck

***examiner's* note** You should be able to explain the attributions you would give to individuals or teams following a variety of results, give practical examples and justify your choices.

Attribution theory III

Q1 Explain the locus-of-control dimension when referring to attributions.

Q2 Attributing failure to unstable factors minimises negative feelings. True or false?

Q3 Explain how inappropriate attributions can contribute to learned helplessness.

Q4 What is attribution retraining?

ANSWERS

the idea that the reasons perceived by a performer for the outcome of his/her actions can affect motivation

A1 The amount of control performers have over the end result, which will affect their personal feelings of pride/satisfaction or shame/guilt

A2 True

A3 Performers may be told that they do not have the ability — an internal stable factor — to improve and as a consequence become demotivated and perceive that they are unable to improve, feeling they will automatically fail at the task

A4 It involves changing the performer's perception of failure, usually from internal stable factors to internal unstable or external factors

***examiner's* note** To maintain a performer's motivation you can attribute failure to any factor other than internal stable factors.

Learned helplessness

Q1 Suggest two reasons why learned helplessness may occur.

Q2 What is general learned helplessness?

Q3 What is specific learned helplessness?

Q4 Outline two strategies to reduce the effects of learned helplessness.

ANSWERS

a feeling that failure is inevitable

A1 Choose from: previous negative experiences; perceived lack of ability; incorrect attributions

A2 A feeling that an attempt at any task linked to an activity or area will fail, e.g. 'I'm poor at any water sports activity'

A3 A feeling that an attempt at a particular task will fail, e.g. anticipating failure when attempting to water-ski but not having the same feeling when confronted with canoeing

A4 Choose from: attribution retraining; positive experiences with success; making the experience enjoyable; giving individual attention; setting realistic task goals; correct use of attributions

***examiner's* note** You should be able to explain the difference between specific and general learned helplessness, the causes of it, and methods for avoidance or elimination.

Stress

Q1 What is the difference between anxiety and eustress?

Q2 What is a stressor?

Q3 Give three examples of stressors that might affect a performer during competition.

Q4 Name the three stages of the general adaptation syndrome.

ANSWERS

the result of individuals perceiving an imbalance between the demands of a task and their ability

A1 Anxiety is a negative emotion caused by an increase in arousal levels; eustress is a positive form of stress which is actively sought by performers to test the limits of their abilities

A2 A demand placed on a performer that initiates stress

A3 Choose from: opposition; nature of the game; result; officials; expectations of others; climate; crowd; frustration with own and others' performance; fear; conflict; media

A4 Alarm reaction; resistance; exhaustion

***examiner's* note** You should be able to explain the general adaptation syndrome and make reference to practical examples in your answer.

Anxiety I

Q1 What is cognitive anxiety?

Q2 What is somatic anxiety?

Q3 Explain the difference between state anxiety and trait anxiety.

Q4 A performer with high levels of A-trait anxiety is more likely to experience higher levels of A-state anxiety. True or false?

ANSWERS

a negative emotion caused by an increase in arousal levels

A1 The thoughts and worries of a performer when confronted by a stressful task

A2 The physiological response of the performer to a stressful task

A3 State anxiety can vary from moment to moment; trait anxiety is the general disposition of a performer to perceive situations as potentially threatening

A4 True

***examiner's* note** You must understand the differences between the various forms of anxiety and be able to explain the characteristics of each and how they influence performance.

Anxiety II

Q1 Give three examples of how a performer might display signs of somatic anxiety.

Q2 What is competitive trait anxiety?

Q3 How might the timing of somatic and cognitive anxiety of a performer differ in the lead-up to a competition?

Q4 How does evaluation apprehension affect a performer's levels of anxiety?

ANSWERS

a negative emotion caused by an increase in arousal levels

A1 Choose from: increased heart rate; sweating; increased respiratory rate; increased blood pressure; increased muscle tension; nausea

A2 The tendency of a performer to view competitive situations as threatening, causing an increase in anxiety levels

A3 Signs of somatic anxiety usually occur close to the event but cognitive anxiety may be experienced for a considerable length of time leading up to the event

A4 As the performer is being judged, this will usually increase his/her arousal and anxiety levels

***examiner's* note** Understand and be able to explain the methods that can be used to control the different forms of anxiety.

Measurement of stress

Q1 Outline the competitive state anxiety inventory (CSAI-2).

Q2 Comment on the validity of the sports competition anxiety test (SCAT).

Q3 Name two physiological tests commonly used to measure levels of stress.

Q4 What is the purpose of testing a performer's level of stress?

ANSWERS

assessing the physical and psychological responses of an individual when in a stress-inducing situation

A1 Self-report questionnaire; series of statements related to the performer's feelings and emotions; measures cognitive anxiety, somatic anxiety and self-confidence in a particular sporting situation

A2 Respondents may lie or give the responses they feel they should; questions may be misinterpreted or inappropriate

A3 Choose from: galvanic skin response; electromyography (EMG); skin temperature; heart rate monitor

A4 Recognition of signs of stress and typical response allows appropriate techniques to be employed to reduce stress levels and improve performance; retesting allows evaluation of success

***examiner's* note** Familiarise yourself with the most commonly used tests. Be able to explain their methodology and evaluate their effectiveness.

Stress management I

Q1 Explain the difference between somatic and cognitive methods of stress management.

Q2 How can cognitive reappraisal lower stress levels?

Q3 How can the technique of imagery be improved so that it can be used effectively to control levels of anxiety?

Q4 What is the difference between internal imagery and external imagery?

ANSWERS

techniques used by performers to lower levels of anxiety and improve performance

A1 Somatic techniques control physiological responses; cognitive techniques control psychological responses

A2 It allows performers to view the situation from a different perspective and re-evaluate their expectations and goals, thus reducing the perceived pressure they may be feeling

A3 Always visualise success; practice regularly; link with realistic goals; develop kinaesthetic feelings; create vivid images; vary the situations

A4 Internal imagery is seeing and feeling yourself completing the movement; external imagery is seeing yourself as others would see you

***examiner's* note** You should be able to list and explain the specific techniques used to control somatic and cognitive anxiety.

Stress management II

Q1 What does the technique of centring involve?

Q2 What is self-talk?

Q3 How is biofeedback used to control levels of stress?

Q4 What is the Jacobsen technique?

ANSWERS

techniques used by performers to lower levels of anxiety and improve performance

A1 It is a breathing technique whereby the performer relaxes his/her chest and shoulder muscles and focuses on the movement of the abdominal muscles while taking deep, slow breaths

A2 A performer developing positive thoughts about his/her performance while eliminating any negative thoughts that might be demotivating

A3 Physiological responses are measured to enable the performer to recognise the best relaxation technique

A4 A form of progressive muscle relaxation, involving tensing and relaxing of specific muscle groups

***examiner's* note** Understand the values and limitations of the different techniques and be able to explain the most appropriate time to use them.

Goal setting

Q1 What do the letters SMARTER represent in terms of goal setting?

Q2 Explain the difference between an outcome goal and a performance goal.

Q3 Why is it important to set short-term and long-term goals?

Q4 Suggest two beneficial effects of goal setting.

ANSWERS

a method of enhancing performance by focusing attention and increasing motivation

A1 S = specific; M = measurable; A = accepted; R = realistic; T = time-phased; E = exciting; R = recorded

A2 An outcome goal refers to the end result and comparison with other performers; a performance goal refers to the performance of individuals compared with their own previous standards and techniques

A3 To provide regular opportunities for success and evaluation, while creating a target to aim for; this maintains motivation levels for an event that may seem distant or unachievable in the short term

A4 Choose from: increases/maintains motivation; focuses attention; develops confidence and self-efficacy; lowers arousal and anxiety

***examiner's* note** Be able to give specific practical examples to highlight the different types of goals and explain which is the most appropriate for different types of performer.

Group dynamics

Q1 Outline the first two stages of group formation.

Q2 The p.................. stage involves individuals working together towards a collective goal.

Q3 How does a group differ from a crowd?

Q4 What does the 'norming' phase of group formation usually involve?

ANSWERS

the interaction among a group of people aiming to solve a problem

A1 Forming — development of new relationships; Storming — conflict between group members while roles are established

A2 Performing

A3 A group has a collective goal; a crowd is a collection of people without a common goal

A4 Once roles within the group have been established, some stability emerges and group members start to work together, developing group cohesion

***examiner's* note** You need to be able to apply the stages of group formation to a practical situation and to outline the characteristics of each stage.

Group performance I

Q1 What is actual productivity?

Q2 Name two common faulty processes that may reduce group productivity.

Q3 What is the potential productivity of a group?

Q4 Suggest three methods that a coach might use to limit faulty processes.

ANSWERS

the effectiveness of the interaction between group members when completing a specific task

A1 Actual productivity = potential productivity – losses due to faulty processes

A2 Coordination losses; motivational losses

A3 The best possible performance given the group's resources that are relevant to the task

A4 Choose from: give positions of responsibility; effective goal setting; feedback; clarify role within the group; extrinsic rewards; video performances; improve fitness levels; develop cohesion (task and social); avoid situations that might lead to social loafing

***examiner's* note** You need to be able to give examples of faulty processes that may occur within a team and to suggest strategies to eradicate or minimise them.

Group performance II

Q1 Give two examples of coordination-faulty processes.

Q2 Give two examples of motivational-faulty processes.

Q3 How might social loafing influence group performance?

Q4 The Ringelmann effect would have a positive impact on group performance. True or false?

ANSWERS

the effectiveness of the interaction between group members when completing a specific task

A1 Choose from: lack of understanding of tactics and strategies; role within the group unclear; poor concentration; poor selective attention

A2 Choose from: lack of intrinsic motivation; lack of extrinsic rewards, e.g. praise, medals; social loafing; Ringelmann effect

A3 It would have a negative influence; the performer would not give maximum effort and would find opportunities to 'hide' within the team, meaning another player would have to cover for him/her

A4 False

***examiner's* note** Make sure you can explain all the terms associated with the 'potential productivity' of a group, with reference to actual examples.

Group performance III

Q1 Suggest why the Ringelmann effect may occur.

Q2 When might a group member be drawn into social loafing?

Q3 Give two methods a coach might use to reduce the effects of social loafing.

Q4 Why is it important for a coach to eliminate social loafers from the group?

ANSWERS

A1 As the group size increases, the performance of an individual may decrease owing to low motivation that results from the loss of individual identity, lack of a clear role and/or reliance on other performers

A2 When individual contribution is not being observed, assessed or valued

A3 Choose from: give positions of responsibility; highlight a specific role; give regular feedback; vary practice; develop fitness levels; avoid situations where social loafing may occur

A4 To avoid a potential faulty process and improve the actual productivity of the group

***examiner's* note** You need to be able to explain the concepts of social loafing, the Ringelmann effect and the implications they have on group productivity.

Group cohesion I

Q1 What is the GEQ and what does it measure?

Q2 What is social cohesion?

Q3 Task cohesion is more important than social cohesion. True or false?

Q4 List three factors that may determine the cohesiveness of a group.

ANSWERS

the tendency of a group to stay together and combine to achieve a common goal

A1 Group environment questionnaire; it measures the cohesiveness of the group in sport-specific situations, in terms of both task cohesion and social cohesion

A2 The interaction of group members in terms of trust, communication and support

A3 True

A4 Choose from: situation; members' characteristics; levels of motivation; leadership style; past experiences

***examiner's* note** You should be able to evaluate the effectiveness of each form of cohesion and the relationship between them.

Group cohesion II

Q1 What is task cohesion?

Q2 Give three methods that a coach may employ to improve group cohesion.

Q3 Name two of Carron's variables, which contribute to group cohesiveness.

Q4 Social cohesion can hinder the performance of a group. True or false?

ANSWERS

the tendency of a group to stay together and combine to achieve a common goal

A1 The effectiveness of the group when working together to complete a task

A2 Choose from: highlight specific roles; team-building exercises; vary practice situations; avoid situations for social loafing; encourage peer support

A3 Choose from: situational/environmental elements; personal elements; team elements; leadership elements

A4 True; e.g. sub-groups with high social cohesion may undermine the integration of the whole group

***examiner's* note** You should understand and be able to explain strategies to improve the cohesion of a group, giving practical examples.

Leadership

Q1 Give the characteristics of a successful leader as proposed by the great man theory.

Q2 What is an emergent leader?

Q3 Social learning theory proposes that leaders can develop through interacting with others. Outline the four stages involved in this process.

Q4 What is a prescribed leader?

ANSWERS

the behavioural process of influencing another individual or group towards achieving a goal

A1 Intelligence, self-confidence, assertion, good looks and a dominating personality

A2 A leader who comes from within the group with the support of team members

A3 Attention — watching a model; retention — creation of a mental picture for future reference; motor reproduction — copying the behaviour of the model; motivation — gaining the level of commitment to repeat the actions (often depends on the reinforcement provided by others)

A4 A leader who is appointed by an external body

***examiner's* note** Social learning theory is relevant to numerous parts of the specification. Learn the different stages of Bandura's model with practical examples of how each can be made more effective.

Leadership style I

Q1 Give the characteristics of an autocratic leader.

Q2 A laissez-faire leadership style is effective when time is limited. True or false?

Q3 Explain how a democratic leader would interact with the group.

Q4 Which form of leadership style encourages interpersonal relationships and is task-orientated?

ANSWERS

the method adopted by a group leader, depending on the situation, group and leader/group relationship

A1 Informs the group of the actions to take; makes all the decisions with no group interaction

A2 False

A3 He/she would encourage the group to discuss the situation, then question members of the group about their ideas and viewpoints and make a final decision based on all the information available

A4 Democratic

***examiner's* note** You need to understand the different forms of leadership and be able to give practical examples of appropriate usage.

Leadership style II

Q1 For what kind of group is a democratic leader suitable?

Q2 When is an autocratic style of leadership most appropriate?

Q3 What often happens when a laissez-faire leader leaves the group to complete a task on its own?

Q4 When left alone, members of a group led by a democratic leader often become aggressive towards each other and rarely complete the task. True or false?

ANSWERS

the method adopted by a group leader, depending on the situation, group and leader/group relationship

A1 Experienced; small; good relationship with coach/leader

A2 Time is limited; the task is difficult/complex/dangerous; large groups; very experienced or novice performers

A3 Poor interaction within the group; sometimes group members become aggressive towards each other, causing them to stray off-task; often they do not complete the activity

A4 False

***examiner's* note** You should be able to suggest which form of leadership style is best for a specific situation and explain the advantages and disadvantages of using a particular style.

Chelladurai's multi-dimensional model of leadership

Q1 Name the three factors that Chelladurai suggested need to be considered when adopting a particular leadership style.

Q2 What are the consequences of all the variants combined?

Q3 What is required behaviour?

Q4 How do actual behaviour and preferred behaviour of a leader differ?

ANSWERS

a theory proposing that numerous factors are considered before deciding on a leadership style

A1 Situational characteristics; leader's characteristics; members' characteristics

A2 These affect the quality of the performance and the levels of satisfaction of the group, which may in turn affect the group's motivation

A3 The type of behaviour necessitated by the situation and nature of the task

A4 Actual behaviour is how the leader instructs the group; preferred behaviour is how the group would like to be treated

***examiner's* note** Familiarise yourself with the multi-dimensional model of leadership. Make sure you can explain the different components and apply them to a practical situation.

Fiedler's contingency model of leadership

Q1 Outline the characteristics of a task-centred/task-oriented leader.

Q2 Outline the characteristics of a relationship/person-oriented leader.

Q3 What does 'favourableness of the situation' mean in this context?

Q4 A task-oriented leader is most effective in moderately favourable conditions. True or false?

ANSWERS

the idea that a leader's effectiveness depends on a combination of personality traits and the situation

A1 Focuses on completing the task; performance is the most important aspect; sets clear goals

A2 Focuses on developing interpersonal relationships; consideration is given to the views and feelings of the group

A3 The relationship between the leader and the group; the leader's position of power and authority; the nature of the task

A4 False

***examiner's* note** You need to be able to give practical examples of when each form of leadership would be most effective and to explain how the situation will affect the leadership style.